NTSB/RAR-11/01
PB2011-916301
Notation 8352
Adopted November 8, 2011

I0413273

Railroad Accident Report

Miami International Airport, Automated People Mover Train
Collision with Passenger Terminal Wall
Miami, Florida
November 28, 2008

**National
Transportation
Safety Board**

490 L'Enfant Plaza, SW
Washington, DC 20594

National Transportation Safety Board. 2011. *Miami International Airport, Automated People Mover Train Collision with Passenger Terminal Wall, Miami, Florida, November 28, 2008.* Railroad Accident Report NTSB/RAR-11/01. Washington, DC.

Abstract: About 4:44 p.m., eastern standard time, on November 28, 2008, a three-car train operating along a fixed guideway on Concourse E at Miami International Airport near Miami, Florida, failed to stop at the passenger platform and struck a wall at the end of the guideway. Although a maintenance technician was monitoring train operations from the lead car of the train when the accident occurred, the train was operating in fully automatic mode without a human operator. The maintenance technician and five passengers on board the train were injured in the accident. One person on the passenger platform also required medical attention.

As a result of its investigation of this accident, the National Transportation Safety Board (NTSB) makes safety recommendations to the U.S. Department of Transportation, to the 50 states and the District of Columbia, to Miami-Dade County, and to Johnson Controls, Inc. The NTSB also reiterates a previously issued safety recommendation to the U.S. Department of Transportation.

The National Transportation Safety Board is an independent Federal agency dedicated to promoting aviation, railroad, highway, marine, pipeline, and hazardous materials safety. Established in 1967, the agency is mandated by Congress through the Independent Safety Board Act of 1974 to investigate transportation accidents, determine the probable causes of the accidents, issue safety recommendations, study transportation safety issues, and evaluate the safety effectiveness of government agencies involved in transportation. The Safety Board makes public its actions and decisions through accident reports, safety studies, special investigation reports, safety recommendations, and statistical reviews.

Recent publications are available in their entirety on the Internet at <http://www.ntsb.gov>. Other information about available publications also may be obtained from the website or by contacting:

National Transportation Safety Board
Records Management Division, CIO-40
490 L'Enfant Plaza, SW
Washington, DC 20594
(800) 877-6799 or (202) 314-6551

Safety Board publications may be purchased, by individual copy or by subscription, from the National Technical Information Service. To purchase this publication, order report number PB2011-916301 from:

National Technical Information Service
5301 Shawnee Road
Alexandria, Virginia 22312
(800) 553-6847 or (703) 605-6000

The Independent Safety Board Act, as codified at 49 U.S.C. Section 1154(b), precludes the admission into evidence or use of Board reports related to an incident or accident in a civil action for damages resulting from a matter mentioned in the report.

Contents

Figures

Acronyms and Abbreviations

APM   automated people mover

ATC   automatic train control

ATO   automatic train operation

ATP   automatic train protection

Bombardier   Bombardier—Automated People Movers

CFR   *Code of Federal Regulations*

DOT   U.S. Department of Transportation

Florida DOT   Florida Department of Transportation

FRA   Federal Railroad Administration

FTA   Federal Transit Administration

JCI   Johnson Controls, Inc.

MARTA   Metropolitan Atlanta Rapid Transit Authority

MDAD   Miami-Dade Aviation Department

mphps   mph per second

NTSB   National Transportation Safety Board

Executive Summary

About 4:44 p.m., eastern standard time, on November 28, 2008, a three-car train operating along a fixed guideway (defined by Title 49 *Code of Federal Regulations* Part 659 as any light, heavy, or rapid rail system, monorail, inclined plane, funicular, trolley, or automated guideway) on E Concourse at Miami International Airport near Miami, Florida, failed to stop at the passenger platform and struck a wall at the end of the guideway. Although a maintenance technician was monitoring train operations from the lead car of the train when the accident occurred, the train was operating in fully automatic mode without a human operator. The maintenance technician and five passengers on board the train were injured in the accident. One person on the passenger platform also required medical attention.

The National Transportation Safety Board determines that the probable cause of this accident was the installation by Johnson Controls, Inc., maintenance technicians of a jumper wire that prevented the overspeed/overshoot system from activating to stop the train when the crystal within the primary program stop module failed. Contributing to the accident were (1) the failure of Johnson Controls, Inc., to provide its maintenance technicians with specific procedures regarding the potential disabling of vital train control systems during passenger operations, (2) ineffective safety oversight by the Miami-Dade Aviation Department, (3) lack of adequate safety oversight of such systems by the state of Florida, and (4) lack of authority by the U.S. Department of Transportation to provide adequate safety oversight of such systems.

The following safety issues were identified during this accident investigation:

- Maintenance procedures and practices of Johnson Controls, Inc.
- Safety oversight of fixed guideway systems.

As a result of this investigation, the National Transportation Safety Board makes safety recommendations to the U.S. Department of Transportation, to the 50 states and the District of Columbia, to Miami-Dade County, and to Johnson Controls, Inc. The National Transportation Safety Board also reiterates a previously issued recommendation to the U.S. Department of Transportation.

1. Factual Information

1.1 The Accident

About 4:44 p.m., eastern standard time, on November 28, 2008, a three-car train operating along a fixed guideway[1] on E Concourse at Miami International Airport near Miami, Florida, failed to stop at the passenger platform and struck a wall at the end of the guideway. Although a maintenance technician was monitoring train operations from the lead car of the train when the accident occurred, the train was operating in fully automatic mode without a human operator. The maintenance technician and five passengers on board the train were injured in the accident. One person on the passenger platform also required medical attention.

The accident occurred at Miami International Airport, which is west of downtown Miami, Florida, and involved a train used to shuttle passengers between two areas of the facility. The accident train was of a type known as an automated people mover (APM) that is normally operated along a fixed guideway in fully automatic mode without a train operator.

The main building at Miami International Airport comprises three contiguous passenger terminals—designated North, Central, and South. Passenger access to planes is via concourses that extend from each of the three terminals, as follows: Concourse D from the North Terminal; Concourses E, F, and G from the Central Terminal; and Concourses H and J from the South Terminal. (See figure 1.)

E Concourse consisted of the main E Concourse and a satellite E Concourse building located about 1,300 feet away. Two three-car APM trains (see figure 2) operated in both directions to shuttle passengers between the main and satellite buildings. Ridership averaged about 9,000 passengers per day.

The trains operated along two parallel 1,360-foot-long concrete guideways running east-west that connected the two concourse buildings. Although the trains were designed to operate automatically, the cars at either end of the train were equipped with operating panels, known as "hostler panels" or "auxiliary control panels," that were normally locked away but that could be accessed and used to operate the trains manually if necessary.

One APM train operated on each guideway. The train operating on the northernmost guideway was designated the "north" train; the other was the "south" train.

---

[1] A *rail fixed guideway system* is defined by Title 49 *Code of Federal Regulations* (CFR) Part 659 as any light, heavy, or rapid rail system, monorail, inclined plane, funicular, trolley, or automated guideway.

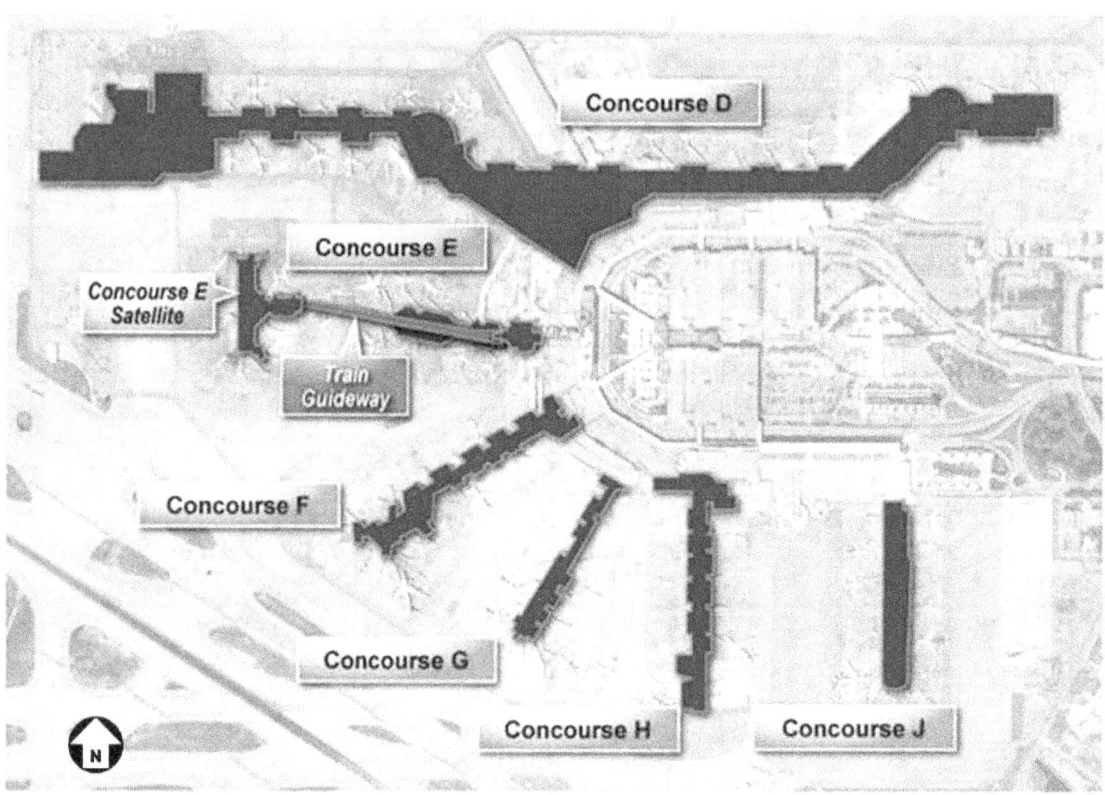

Figure 1. Aerial view of the Miami International Airport.

Figure 2. APM trains of the type involved in this accident. In this view, looking west toward Satellite E, the south train is on the left.

Train operations were typically configured such that one train would be loading and unloading passengers at the main building while the other was loading and unloading at the satellite building. The trip between the two buildings generally took about 1 minute, with a 45-second (adjustable) dwell time at either end before the trains reversed direction toward the other station.

During the weeks leading up to the accident, the south train had recurring technical problems (discussed later in this report) that caused it to occasionally lose electrical traction power and stop along the guideway in mid-route between the two buildings. When this occurred, a Johnson Controls, Inc., (JCI) maintenance technician[2] would go out to the train and either restore it to automatic operation or, using the hostler panel in the lead car, operate the train manually into the station.

On November 28, 2008, JCI maintenance technicians were taking turns riding the south train in 1-hour shifts to ensure a fast recovery in the event that the train stopped on the guideway. The hostler panels were left unlocked to expedite the recovery process if manual operation was required. Just before the accident, at the satellite building, a shift lead maintenance technician and a second JCI maintenance technician finished their 1-hour shift on board the south train and were relieved by a single JCI maintenance technician. After the shift change, the south train departed the satellite building with the maintenance technician occupying the lead car. He told investigators that he was alone in the car. Three passengers were in the middle car, and two were in the last car.

The accident occurred about 4:44 p.m., eastern standard time. The maintenance technician on board stated that instead of stopping at its platform location at the main E Concourse station, the train continued past the berthing point at the station and struck the wall of the concourse building. The maintenance technician said that as a result of the impact, he was knocked down, after which the lights in the car went out. He said he used the emergency handle and opened the car door to walk out. He recalled hearing people yelling for help and also heard personnel from the train operations control room calling him on the radio. He said he used his cell phone to contact the operations control room and then began opening the doors to the remaining cars. The APM was not equipped with any onboard event recorders, nor were they required. A security video camera atop gate D47, although not capturing the accident, did capture the train entering the station just before the accident. A study of the video footage showed that the train entered the station at about 20 mph without decelerating to prepare for stopping at its berthing point.

1.2 Emergency Response

At 4:47 p.m., the JCI maintenance technician on board the accident train contacted operations control room personnel by telephone, notifying them of the collision and requesting that medical assistance be dispatched. Incident logs indicate that the Miami-Dade County Fire Rescue Department and the Miami-Dade County Police Department were then notified. Police

---

[2] As will be discussed later in this report, JCI, in January 2008, had contracted with the Miami-Dade Aviation Department (MDAD) to maintain the APM system at the airport.

records indicate that personnel were dispatched at 4:49 p.m. and arrived on scene at 4:51 p.m. Fire department rescue units 12 and 2, along with Engine 12, arrived on scene shortly thereafter.

Four of the injured train passengers were transported to Metropolitan Hospital. One passenger was transported to Jackson Memorial Hospital, and one person on the passenger platform was transported to Hialeah Hospital. One passenger was seriously injured. Two others were found to have minor injuries, and two passengers were treated and released. The maintenance technician, who was on the train at the time of the accident, initially refused medical attention but later went to his personal physician because he was experiencing discomfort. The passenger listed in serious condition was released from the hospital within 3 days.

1.3 Damages

Damages to the south train were initially estimated at $15 to $16 million for replacement of the train and the necessary wayside adjustments. This estimate was based on finding used equipment from a different property that could replace the south train. A replacement train could not be found to replace the south train; therefore, the north train has been the only train operating since the accident.

1.4 Mechanical Equipment Description

The APM equipment operating on the E Concourse guideways originally consisted of two semipermanently joined cars (designated the A-car and B-car) with a capacity of 75 passengers per car. Later, to provide additional passenger capacity, a third car (C-car) was added between the A- and B-cars. The three-car trains were 107.7 feet long.

The A- and B-cars were equipped with hostler panels for manual operation, but the only active hostler panel was the one on the lead car (which could be either the A- or B-car, depending on train direction). The manual controls were secured behind a locked panel at the outboard end of each of those cars. Each JCI maintenance technician and JCI supervisor had keys to the doors securing the manual controls.

Train travel was centered along each guideway through use of steel guiderails affixed along the center of the guideways. (See figure 3.) The trains rode on rubber tires, with each car powered by a three-phase, 480-volt d.c. traction motor. Top speed was designed to be 26 mph but was limited to 22 mph. Braking was provided through interconnected dynamic brake[3] and friction brake systems on each car. The braking systems were blended to provide initial deceleration from the dynamic brake system, with supplemental braking provided by the friction brake system. The friction brake system provides for both normal and emergency functions. As designed, the dynamic brakes would have provided the majority of the normal braking. The friction brake is applied by mechanical pressure from a spring. When the APM is in operation,

---

[3] In *dynamic* braking, the train car's traction motors are converted to electric generators driven by kinetic energy from the moving car. The generated electricity flows into a resistor grid, which creates an electrical "load" on the traction motor/generator. This load acts to slow the motor shaft rotation, resulting in a braking action being applied to the train wheels.

the spring is pneumatically compressed, thereby, releasing the friction brake. An intentional application of the friction brake under normal operations, known as a service application, is accomplished by gradually releasing the pressure in the brake cylinder to apply a controlled service braking application. An emergency application is triggered when the vital automatic train protection (ATP) subsystem detects any potentially unsafe condition (such as overspeed) and disengages the automatic train operation (ATO) pneumatic control of the friction brakes, causing the brakes to be spring applied. The ATP subsystem is described in section 1.5 and illustrated in figure 5. Normal deceleration was designed to be 2.0 mph per second (mphps). Emergency deceleration was designed to be 3.0 mphps.

Figure 3. APM north train guideway looking toward the main terminal.

1.5 Train Control System Description

An automatic train control (ATC) system incorporated the command, control, and communication equipment necessary for operating the E Concourse APMs without the need of an operator. The functions of the ATC system were carried out by three subsystems, as follows:

Automatic Train Operation: Performed basic operating functions within the safety constraints of the ATP subsystem. (See figure 4.)

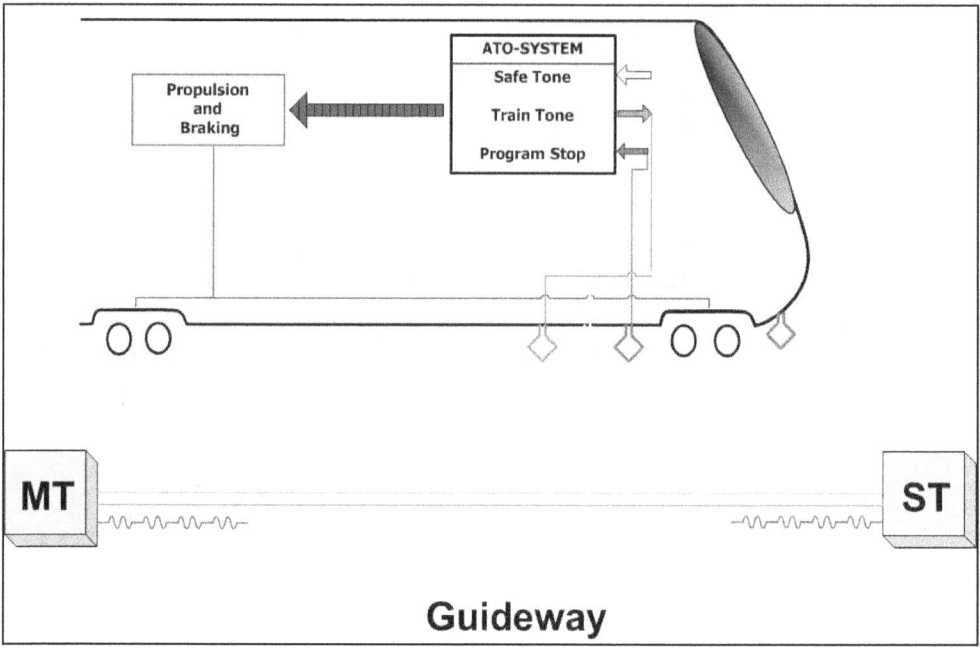

Figure 4. Automatic train operation block diagram.

Automatic Train Protection: Performed safety-critical functions that removed propulsion power and applied train brakes when the system exceeded safe operating parameters of the ATO subsystem. (See figure 5.)

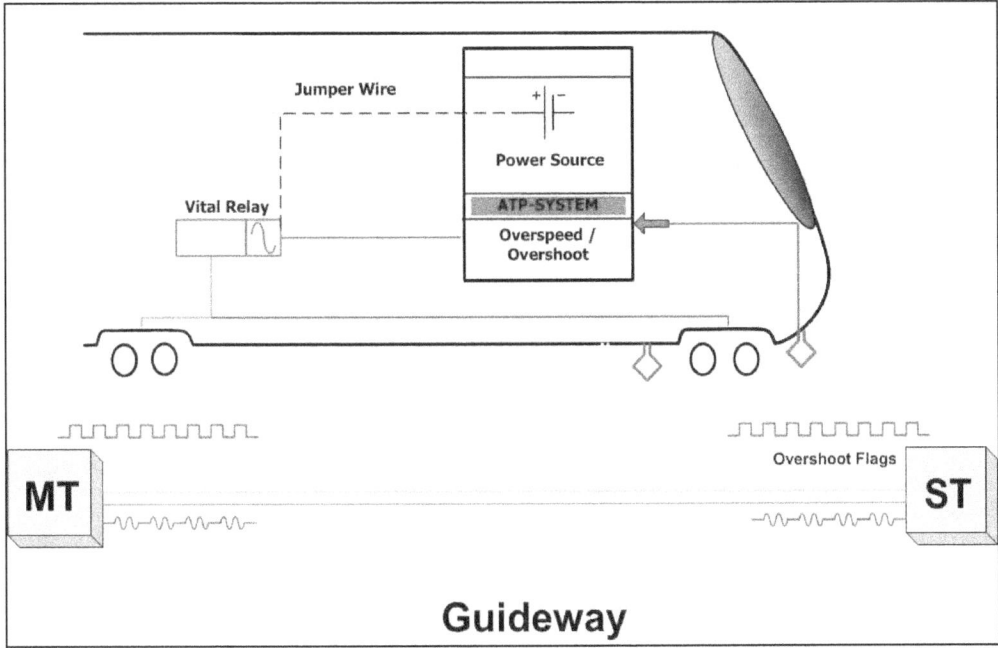

Figure 5. Automatic train protection block diagram.

Automatic Train Supervision: Provided for supervision of the APM system by operations control room computers as well as provided for manual intervention/override by central train control personnel if necessary. (See figure 6.)

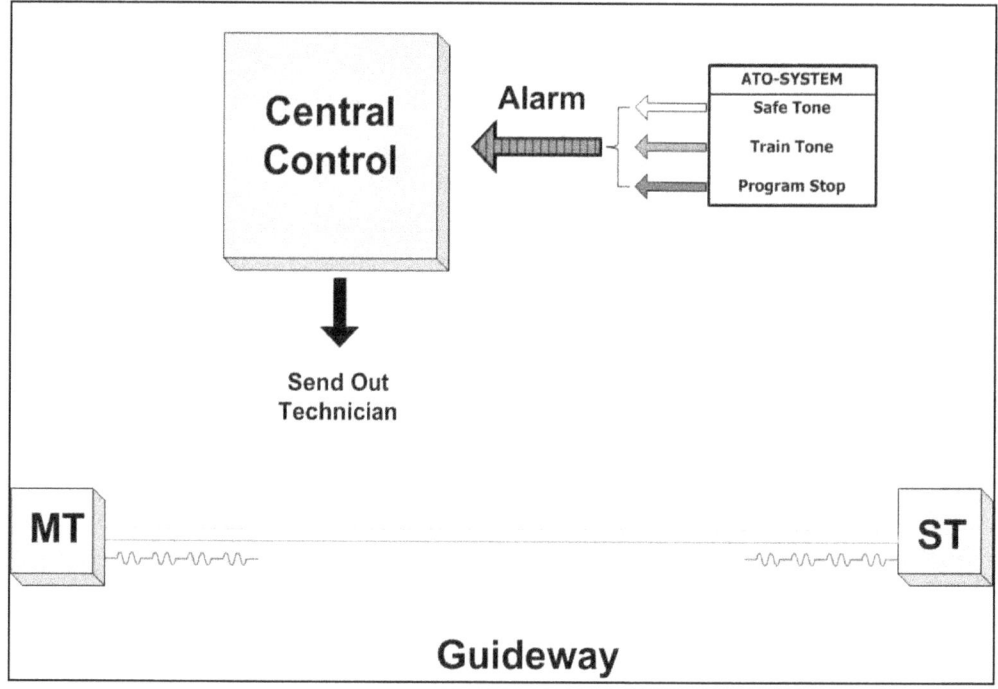

Figure 6. Automatic train supervision block diagram.

Electronic train control components at the stations and along the wayside performed a number of automated functions, including providing commands to the trains on both guideways, receiving information from the trains, controlling wayside door operation, and interfacing with the ATC power control equipment that ran the trains.

1.5.1 Train Tone

Two sets of parallel wires spaced 2 inches apart ran the entire length of each guideway. One set of wires served as a wayside inductive loop antenna that received a tone signal from a train as it moved along the guideway and while berthed at the stations. This "train tone" signal was transmitted at all times unless an Alarm 1 was detected. An Alarm 1 was caused whenever (1) the train lost verification that the ground pick-up shoes were in contact with the ground rail, or (2) any door on the train opened when the train was not properly stopped in a station. Loss of the train tone caused the power rails to be disconnected from the 480-volt source and generated visual and audible alarms in the operations control room.

1.5.2 Safe Tone

Another set of parallel wires served as a wayside inductive loop antenna that transmitted a "safe tone" signal to the train. Two frequencies were used for the safe tone signal, which the train interpreted as a command to move toward one station or the other, depending on the frequency. Loss of the safe tone signal caused the train to stop or prevented it from moving. Loss of the safe tone also generated alarms in the operations control room.

1.5.3 Program Stop

APM station stops were controlled by the "program stop" system, a nonvital[4] train positioning system that controlled the speed of a train as it approached a station and properly positioned the train in the station so that the train doors aligned with the wayside station doors. The program stop system was a function of the ATO subsystem. Four wayside inductive loop antennas, one at the approach to each station, transmitted to the trains a program stop signal that was used as a location reference to control deceleration and to provide for precise stopping.

The program stop antennas did not run the length of the guideways but instead extended from the normal station stopping points (berthing points) to a point 575 feet away, near the station entrances. The antenna wires were spaced 2 inches apart and crossed every 12 inches, thereby forming a series of 1-foot loops. A program stop signal was turned on before a train departed the station at one end of the guideway. When a train approached within 575 feet of a station and began to pass over the program stop antenna, a receiver antenna on board the train picked up the induced stop signal. The phase (polarity) of this signal changed with each loop of the antenna. A program stop module on board the train counted these phase changes to determine the train's location relative to the stopping point. When the train arrived at the station, the program stop signal was turned off at that station and turned on at the other station for the return trip.

The ATO subsystem verified the presence of a stop signal before the train departed a station and while the train was in transit. Loss of verification of the program stop signal caused the safe tone signal to be turned off, which would stop a train or prevent it from moving and would generate alarms in the operations control room.

1.5.4 Overspeed/Overshoot System

The "overshoot" system was the vital (safety-critical), fail-safe[5] logic of the emergency braking system. The overshoot system was an ATP function. Two rows of electronic overshoot "flags" were set along each guideway on the approach to the stopping point at a station. The flag system worked by activating sensors on the train as the train passed over the flags. The time that elapsed between these sensor activations indicated train velocity. If a train was traveling faster than the allowed speed, the ATP system would automatically apply the friction brakes to safely stop the train.

---

[4] *Nonvital* refers to any system or circuit, the function of which does not affect the safety of train operations (because of the presence of a *vital* system or circuit that is designed to activate to prevent an accident).

[5] *Fail-safe* is a design philosophy applied to safety-critical systems. The fail-safe principle requires that a system be prohibited from assuming an unsafe state in the event of a component failure.

1.6 Operations Control Room

APM train operations were monitored from the operations control room, which was staffed by personnel from MDAD. Alarms were indicated both visually and audibly. Some of these alarms could be reset in the operations control room by MDAD personnel; others required that a JCI maintenance technician be dispatched to the train.

1.7 Operation and Maintenance of the APM System

Westinghouse Electric was the original equipment manufacturer and installer of the Miami International Airport APM train system, which began operation in 1980. Through mergers and acquisitions, the original equipment manufacturer became Bombardier–Automated People Movers (Bombardier).[6] The original equipment manufacturer was initially awarded contracts to both operate and maintain the system. Later, MDAD employees staffed the operations control room, and only the maintenance of the system was contracted to Bombardier and its predecessor companies. The maintenance contract was extended for 28 years.

When Bombardier's last regular maintenance contract expired in February 2007, the company rejected the contract extension offered by the Dade County Board of Commissioners. Bombardier indicated that it would extend the maintenance contract only if significant changes were made regarding limitations of liability. The company's stated concern was that the trains were past their design life. Miami-Dade County declined changing the limitations of liability; therefore, both parties agreed to extend the contract termination date to July 31, 2007. MDAD advertised for a competitive bid to award a new maintenance contract for the APM system and Bombardier submitted a bid for this new contract.

In April 2007, Bombardier raised concerns with MDAD about the safety of the APM system. Experts from Bombardier, Miami-Dade Transit,[7] and consultants hired by MDAD were assembled to evaluate the condition of the APM system. The running surfaces of the guideways were found to need repairs, which were carried out by Miami-Dade Transit. The MDAD consultants found cracks in the train underbodies but concluded that, if the cracks were repaired, the trains could continue to operate safely for 5 additional years.

On July 24, 2007, the county awarded Bombardier an interim agreement under which Bombardier would operate and maintain the APM system for an additional 6 months (expiring at midnight on January 28, 2008.) In August 2007, MDAD issued an invitation to bid for the contract to maintain the APM system. During the bidding process, MDAD determined that Bombardier and JCI were both qualified bidders.[8] JCI would assume responsibility for maintaining the system beginning on January 29, 2008.

---

[6] Westinghouse Electric went through several mergers and acquisitions: AEG Westinghouse Transportation Systems; ADTranz/ABB Daimler-Benz Transportation; Daimler Chrysler Rail Systems; and Bombardier.

[7] Miami-Dade Transit, a department of Miami-Dade County government, is responsible for planning and providing all public transit services in the county.

[8] *Qualified bidder* refers to a potential bidder who meets the minimum standards of experience, financial ability, managerial ability, reputation, and work history for a project in question.

Bombardier representatives told investigators that in early January 2008 they provided MDAD with a letter outlining the anticipated hand-over process between Bombardier and MDAD. The contract did not require that Bombardier train a third party before the expiration of the contract.

The Bombardier transition team worked with MDAD and its consultant, and a hand-over process was agreed upon. Bombardier provided National Transportation Safety Board (NTSB) investigators with records indicating that all of the elements of that process were signed off by MDAD and its consultant. Bombardier indicated that MDAD allowed JCI personnel to be on site before Bombardier's contract expired on January 28, 2008. No contract provision provided for a joint Bombardier-JCI maintenance activity. JCI personnel did not work alongside Bombardier personnel to become familiar with the system before taking over responsibility for its maintenance. Once the new contract became effective, JCI employed a site business manager and nine maintenance technicians to maintain the equipment and ensure that it was operational. The site business manager for Miami airport's APM had worked for JCI for about 10 months. Prior to joining JCI, he had worked for about 10 years as a safety engineer and as a quality engineer at the Metropolitan Atlanta Rapid Transit Authority (MARTA). Prior to MARTA, he previously had worked at the Miami airport's APM for over 15 years as a maintenance technician for Bombardier and its predecessor companies. Three of the nine maintenance technicians who were hired by JCI were initially Bombardier employees who maintained the Miami airport APM system.

The new JCI maintenance technicians had backgrounds in electrical or electronic systems and were provided with on-the-job training for several months. Maintenance technicians who completed the training and passed a test were considered qualified to operate an APM train and perform maintenance on the system. JCI maintenance technicians were required to submit to preemployment drug testing, but neither JCI personnel nor MDAD operations control room personnel were covered under any postaccident drug/alcohol toxicology testing policy or random drug/alcohol toxicology testing policy. There were no hours-of-service requirements for any of the job positions involved with the APM train system.

1.8 Events Preceding the Accident

According to JCI personnel, in the weeks preceding the accident, the south train had been experiencing recurring failures with (1) the wayside antenna system for the train tone signal, (2) the dynamic braking system, and (3) the overspeed/overshoot feature. In the process of troubleshooting the train tone signal, maintenance technicians found that the antenna wires were brittle and, in some areas, broken. They replaced the wayside antenna, but after the installation, they continued working on the antenna alignment because the south train was still losing traction power and stopping on the guideway. The stopped train required that a JCI maintenance technician go out to the train to reset the alarm. Maintenance technicians were being routinely assigned to ride the trains during periods of passenger service in attempts to diagnose and correct the various problems and to be in place to quickly assist in recovering the train in the event of an en route failure.

One week before the accident, on November 21, 2008, the second-shift lead maintenance technician installed a jumper wire between two terminals on a terminal board in the system control compartment of the A-car of the south train. The maintenance technician indicated that the jumper wire was installed to keep the train in service while work continued toward identifying the failures that were causing the train to stop. JCI staff kept a logbook that detailed maintenance activities for each shift. The JCI manager stated he reviewed this log at the beginning of each day and discussed the entries with his staff. An entry for the third shift on November 21, 2008, stated: "Jumpered [terminals] TBB-5 to TBL-14 to put train back in service." Based on log entries, interviews, and the postaccident mechanical inspection (discussed later in this report), the jumper wire remained in place during regular operations of the south train from November 21 until the accident on November 28.

The JCI site business manager, the shift leader, and JCI maintenance technicians all stated they were aware that the jumper wire was in place, but they gave differing answers to questions about the internal authority to apply the jumper wire and about whether the jumper wire was to be applied only during testing or if it was to remain in place during regular passenger service. The lead maintenance technician said that he did not know why the jumper wire was used, but he recalled a previous problem on the north train that was solved with a jumper wire. He said that the site business manager had directed that the jumper wire be installed to put the south train back in service. The site business manager stated that the jumper wire was used to provide 24 volts to the hostler panel, which he said he believed was not getting power to operate the train. He further stated that he ordered the shift lead maintenance technician not to use the jumper wire when trains were in passenger service.

A JCI maintenance technician told investigators that after the jumper wire was installed on November 21, he reviewed the circuit schematics and tested the south train. He concluded that the jumper wire bypassed the safety-critical overspeed/overshoot relay and would, thus, allow the train to continue past the overshoot position and contact the bumping post in the event of a failure of the program stop system. He said that he informed the shift lead maintenance technician who had installed the jumper wire, but was told to leave the jumper wire in place so the train could continue to operate. The investigation determined that JCI had no formalized, written maintenance procedures to guide maintenance technicians working on or around vital train control system components.

1.9 Postaccident Inspection and Testing

1.9.1 Braking System

The at-rest position of the damaged train (south train) did not allow for a detailed inspection of the undercarriage and associated braking equipment. For the week prior to the accident, the JCI reports and JCI work records indicated an ongoing problem with the brake system on the south train. The smell of overheated braking material had been evident, and a cool down period at the end of each run was in place. Because the dynamic brakes were not functioning, the train had to rely solely on its friction brake system to slow and to stop. Hence, the friction brake system was overheating. JCI implemented a cool-down period for this train to allow its brake system to cool.

According to JCI staff, no stopping tests had been conducted on either train before the accident because of concerns about stress being placed on their aging undercarriages. On December 7, 2008, the NTSB-led investigative team conducted a series of stopping tests using the north train, with the following results:

Test 1 – The emergency stop button was activated while the train was moving at full speed in automatic operation. The train stopped in 83 feet 3 inches. Alarm 1 sounded at the operations control room. Maintenance technicians were able to recover the train manually and move the train forward. In this test, the train stopped as expected and performed within design parameters.

Test 2 – The test simulated the opening of a passenger door while the train was moving at full speed in automatic operation. The train stopped smoothly in 202 feet 10 inches. Alarm 1 sounded at the operations control room. Maintenance technicians were able to recover the train manually and move the train forward. In this test, the train stopped as expected and performed within design parameters.

Test 3 – Attempts were made to test the response of a train if it entered the station and approached the berthing point while operating at greater than 7 mph in manual mode. Anticipated results were that the overspeed/overshoot system would go into emergency stop and apply the friction brakes to stop the train. On the two attempts when all the test parameters were met, an overspeed emergency application was initiated, and the train stopped short of the bumping post. As designed, no dynamic or service brakes were applied, and the emergency stop was accomplished solely with the friction brakes, which was expected.

Test 4 – The train was operated manually from the berthing position toward the bumping post at a speed below 3 mph. Anticipated results were that the train would go into emergency stop within 4 feet of the overshoot flags. The train went into emergency application and stopped within the designated parameters.

Test 5 – While the train was operated manually, the overshoot/override system was manually activated. Anticipated results were that the train should not travel at a speed greater than 3 mph. The train was able to move but not at a speed greater than 3 mph, which was within the design parameters.

In summary, the north train performed as intended and safely stopped in all the brake test situations. The results of the five tests were performed without a jumper wire, and the train operated within design parameters.

1.9.2 Train Control System

NTSB investigators inspected the system control compartment of the lead car (A-car) of the south train after the accident. A jumper wire was found to be in place on the terminal board between terminal locations TBB-5 and TBL-14. (See figure 7.) Because of damage to the south train, investigators were unable to test the train control system with the jumper wire in place. A review of the electric circuit schematics revealed that the jumper wire was bypassing the circuit that controlled electrical energy to the coil of the vital overspeed/overshoot relay. In case of a failure of the program stop module, the circuit was designed to cut electrical power to the overspeed/overshoot relay coil, causing it to command an emergency stop. The jumper wire provided direct voltage to the coil, which kept the vital relay energized and prevented it from commanding a stop when the program stop module failed.

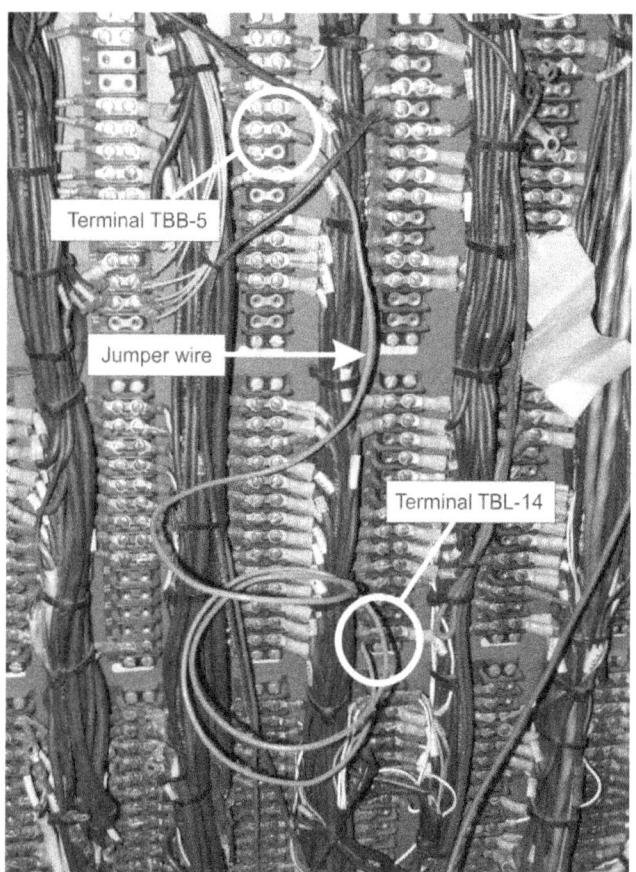

Figure 7. Train control terminal board as found after the accident with a jumper wire in place.

Postaccident measurements on the south guideway determined that the program stop signal was being transmitted within acceptable parameters to the south train. In addition, the overshoot flag system was verified to be wired in series and to exhibit full continuity. The overshoot flag system was removed and examined, and no exceptions were noted.

The electro-mechanical vital overspeed/overshoot relay mounted within the system control compartment onboard the accident train was also removed for testing. The tag on the relay indicated it was last tested on December 4, 2001. The relay was bench tested on February 25, 2009, at Bombardier facilities in Pittsburgh, Pennsylvania. Test results indicated the relay was performing within the manufacturer's specifications.

Investigators also removed the program stop module from the accident train for testing. The investigation revealed ongoing concerns by MDAD, JCI, and Bombardier about how to test the program stop modules because the testing required a unique testing device. Bombardier had such a device and had used it routinely during the time the company maintained the trains to validate the modules and to make any necessary repairs and modifications. JCI was in the process of acquiring spare program stop modules as well as a testing device for the modules; however, at the time of the accident, JCI did not have access to either of these devices.

On December 17, 2008, investigators conducted a series of tests on several program stop modules at the Miami airport APM train maintenance facility. The tests were conducted using a prototype testing device that allowed for signal stimulation of a program stop module and for monitoring for positive connection. Preliminary tests were conducted on known serviceable and defective modules in order to confirm the ability of the prototype test device to generate valid test results. The results of these tests validated the device.

Investigators removed the program stop module that was in place on the south train at the time of the accident and tested it using the prototype test device. The module completely failed the first receiver dynamic test. The binary input indicated "signal is absent." The module was then tested to determine where the signal was lost. The testing revealed that the commutating filter had failed. That filter consisted of two components—an integrated circuit and a crystal—that together formed an oscillator. This oscillator was designed to count the phase changes in the program stop antenna to determine the train's location in relation to its berthing point. The failed commutating filter on the south train could not count the changes, which essentially disabled the program stop system.

Because of the results of this testing and the fact that the results were derived through use of a prototype test apparatus, Bombardier used its specialized test device to retest the south train program stop module at the company's facility in Pittsburgh. The testing confirmed that the commutating filter crystal was inoperative.

1.10 JCI Maintenance Practices and Procedures

JCI had no written policies or procedures regarding maintenance activities that had the potential to bypass critical circuits. No procedures were in place to delineate the use of jumper wires while troubleshooting or while trains were in passenger service.

According to JCI staff, JCI maintenance technicians had not conducted stopping tests on either train before the accident. Staff members initially told investigators that they had no procedures for conducting tests of the emergency braking system. JCI provided the NTSB with a form indicating that some type of braking test was being conducted. The form provided no procedures for a thorough brake test, including tests of emergency braking. Records showed that the most recent brake test had been performed on November 18, 2008. A review of the materials that Bombardier had turned over to JCI with the transfer of the maintenance contract revealed detailed procedures for testing the train brakes. JCI managers said that brake tests were not being routinely conducted because of concerns that the tests would place undue stress on the trains' aging undercarriages.

The APM equipment manufacturer had recommended that vital relays on board its trains be tested every 4 years. The overspeed/overshoot system's vital relay, which was bypassed by a jumper wire, was tagged indicating that it was last inspected on December 4, 2001. JCI could not document any test procedures for the APM vital relays. Neither Bombardier nor JCI could provide test records nor were they required to do so due to the absence of mandatory recordkeeping requirements.

1.11 Safety Oversight of Fixed Guideway Systems

1.11.1 Federal Oversight

The U.S. Department of Transportation (DOT) consists of 11 individual operating administrations, one of which is the Federal Railroad Administration (FRA). The FRA promulgates and enforces railroad safety regulations, administers railroad assistance programs, conducts research and development to support improved railroad safety and policy, and consolidates government support of rail transportation activities.

The FRA governs the operation of standard-gage railroads that are part of the general railroad system of transportation such as freight, intercity passenger, and commuter railroads. Except under some very limited and clearly defined circumstances, the FRA does not regulate any urban rapid transit operation that is not connected with the general railroad system. The FRA enforces compliance with Federal regulations regarding hazardous materials, motive power and equipment, operating practices, track, and signal and train control. Within these five disciplines, detailed regulations provide for the safe operation of a railroad. FRA regulations cover areas such as locomotive safety standards; event recorder standards; passenger car equipment design and crashworthiness standards; control of drug and alcohol use; hours of service; passenger train emergency preparedness; qualification and certification of locomotive engineers; track standards; and the installation, inspection, maintenance, and repair of signal and train control systems.

The Federal Transit Administration (FTA) is another administration within the DOT. Through its grant programs, the FTA helps plan, build, and operate transit systems. Unlike the FRA, however, the FTA does not have statutory authority to promulgate safety regulations. In its enabling legislation, the FTA is prohibited from regulating the operations of a transit agency.

Over time, the Congress provided the FTA with regulatory authority in two areas: drug and alcohol use[9] and state safety oversight.[10] Although the FTA's Office of Safety and Security is responsible for administration of the drug/alcohol and state safety oversight programs, the FTA has no direct enforcement authority of these regulations.

Under the FTA's state safety oversight regulation, each state is required to establish an oversight agency to carry out the oversight responsibilities specified in Part 659. The state oversight agency, which must be a state agency other than the transit agency itself, is charged with ensuring that each FTA-funded rail transit agency within that state develops and implements a safety management program that is consistent with the requirements of the

---

[9] Public Law 102-143, title V, section 6. The Omnibus Transportation Employee Testing Act of 1991. Act of October 28, 1991. 49 U.S.C. 5331. The FTA's implementing regulations, "Prevention of Alcohol Misuse and Prohibited Drug Use in Transit Operations," are codified in 49 CFR Part 655.

[10] Public Law 102-240, section 3029. The Intermodal Surface Transportation Efficiency Act of 1991. Act of December 18, 1991. 49 U.S.C. 5330. The FTA's implementing regulations, "Rail Fixed Guideway Systems: State Safety Oversight," are codified in 49 CFR Part 659.

regulation. The APM at Miami International Airport does not receive any FTA funding and is therefore not covered by Part 659. Each rail transit system is also permitted to develop its own internal procedures, rules, and standards governing operating practices and maintenance standards. The oversight agency is limited by the regulation to reviewing the program submitted by the rail transit agency. The ability to develop and enforce safety regulations is limited to the authority granted by each state's legislature.

1.11.2 State of Florida Oversight

Florida's Department of Transportation (Florida DOT) is designated by state statutes as the oversight agency with the responsibility for implementing and enforcing the statutory provisions statewide. Section 341.061 of the Florida statutes describes a fixed guideway transportation system as a transit system for the transporting of people by a conveyance specifically designed for travel on a stationary rail or other guideway, whether located on, above, or under the ground. These systems include commuter rail, heavy or rapid rail transit, light rail transit, streetcar, monorail, automated guideway transit, inclined plane, and APM. Any fixed guideway transportation system that is totally or partially financed with state funds is subject to the standards, procedures, and technical direction outlined in the *State Safety and Security Oversight Program Standards Manual*.

The Florida DOT designates two categories of fixed guideway transportation systems. The first category is a non-FTA-funded fixed guideway transportation system and includes any system, whether private or government-owned, operating in Florida and financed wholly or in part by state funds and subject to statute section 341.061. The second category is a FTA-funded fixed guideway transportation system and includes any system subject to section 341.061 of the statutes and 49 CFR Part 659 of the Federal regulations. The following lists the transit agencies under the Florida DOT:

	Transportation System
Non-FTA funded	South Florida Regional Transportation Authority Tri-Rail Commuter Rail
	Orlando International Airport Automated People Mover System
	Tampa International Airport Automated People Mover System
FTA funded	Miami-Dade Transit Agency Metro-Rail and Metro-Mover
	Jacksonville Transportation Authority Skyway
	Hillsborough Area Regional Transit Authority – TECO Line Streetcar

On December 7, 1987, the Florida DOT requested that a system safety program plan be developed for the Miami International Airport APM train system. MDAD replied by letter on February 26, 1988. The letter acknowledged that the Florida DOT participated in the financing of the system through an agreement with Dade County and that the system was designed and constructed "in close coordination with a Florida DOT engineer and project manager from the Tallahassee office." The letter further stated that section 341.061 of the Florida statute was not adopted until 1984 and amended in 1986. The letter stated that section 341.061 was not retroactive and therefore did not apply to the Miami International Airport APM system. In the letter, MDAD concluded that development of a system safety program plan for the APM system at the Miami International Airport was not required. The investigation revealed no record of subsequent correspondence or communication between the state of Florida and MDAD with regard to safety oversight of the Miami airport APM system.

1.11.3 Miami-Dade County Oversight

MDAD operated the Miami International Airport for Miami-Dade County. The MDAD Facilities Maintenance Division was responsible for oversight of the APM system contractor. The MDAD project manager/superintendent of contracts and construction was responsible for monitoring the safety and maintenance of the system. The MDAD project manager/superintendent worked as needed with a consulting firm on issues concerning the APM system.

As previously discussed, at the time of the accident, the maintenance of the APM system was contracted to JCI. The maintenance contract required that if any vehicle had a malfunction that significantly degraded passenger comfort or safety, it must be taken out of service until all of the systems were fully restored to normal operation. The contract further required that until a malfunctioning system was repaired and restored to normal operation, the system should operate with one train.

1.12 APM Standards

The Automated People Mover Standards Committee of the American Society of Civil Engineers developed a minimum set of standards[11] in 1996 (revised in 2005) to establish requirements to operate an APM system at an acceptable level of safety and performance. The APM standards are written in four parts. Part 1 covers the minimum requirements for the operating environment, safety requirements, system dependability, ATC, audio and visual communications, and system and safety program requirements. Part 2 provides information on vehicles and propulsion and braking systems. Part 3 covers the topics of electrical equipment, stations, and guideways. Part 4 covers security, emergency preparedness, system verification and demonstration, operations, maintenance and training, and operational monitoring. The standards are not mandatory and are intended to assist the industry.

---

[11] American National Standards Institute/American Society of Civil Engineers/Transportation & Development Institute Standards 21-05, 21.2-08, 21.3-08, and 21.4-08.

2. Analysis

2.1 The Accident

At the time of the accident, the APM south train was operating, as designed, in fully automatic mode. Although a JCI maintenance technician was on board who could have operated the train manually if it had stopped unexpectedly, the maintenance technician was essentially a passenger so long as the train continued to function normally.

In automatic mode, the train depended for its safe operation on the proper functioning of the various ATC components and subsystems. For example, as the train neared its berthing point at either end of the guideway, onboard receivers would detect a signal induced from the wayside program stop antenna. The program stop module on board the train was designed to count the phase changes in the loops of the wayside antenna to determine the train's location with regard to the stopping point. The ATC system would then decelerate and apply necessary braking to ensure a safe stop. If a component of the program stop system failed, the overspeed/overshoot system was designed to intervene to stop the train.

In the case of the south train on November 28, 2008, the program stop system failed. But because of a jumper wire that had been installed by JCI maintenance technicians, the vital overspeed/overshoot system could not function as designed, thus removing the fail-safe feature of the ATC system. This allowed the south train to continue past its normal berthing point and strike the wall of the E Concourse main building.

2.2 Program Stop System

Postaccident testing of the wayside program stop antenna indicated that the antenna was properly transmitting the stop signal to the south train. Testing of the program stop module from the south train, however, revealed a failed crystal in the program stop module oscillator, which rendered the oscillator inoperative. The oscillator was the component within the stop module that was responsible for counting the phase changes in the wayside loop antenna to determine the train's proximity to its berthing point. Without a properly functioning oscillator, the train control system had no means of effecting a normal deceleration and stop. The fact that the train had made normal stops during previous trips indicates that failure occurred without warning after its most recent station stop. The NTSB concludes that the south train failed to make a normal deceleration and stop at its station platform berthing point because of the failure of a crystal within the program stop system module.

2.3 Overspeed/Overshoot System

In the event of a failure of the type evidenced by the south train program stop module on the day of the accident, the overspeed/overshoot system should have functioned as a backup system to prevent the accident. Postaccident testing showed the wayside overshoot flags were working normally. Additionally, the electro-mechanical overspeed/overshoot relay mounted on the south train was tested and found to be performing within the manufacturer's specifications.

The investigation revealed, however, that JCI maintenance technicians, while troubleshooting ongoing problems with the ATC system and in order to keep the trains in service, had installed a jumper wire in the train control compartment of the south train. The NTSB reviewed the system schematics and determined that this jumper wire bypassed the overspeed/overshoot system relay. Bypassing the relay took the fail-safe component of the system "out of the loop" and placed sole responsibility for safely stopping the train on the nonvital program stop system—with no backup system in place if that system failed. Postaccident examination of train control and train braking system components revealed no evidence to suggest that the overspeed/overshoot system would not have worked as designed on the day of the accident. The NTSB concludes that, had it not been bypassed by placement of a jumper wire as part of a troubleshooting process, the overspeed/overshoot relay on board the south train would have functioned as designed when the program stop module failed and the overspeed/overshoot system would have intervened to safely stop the train and prevent the accident.

2.4 JCI Maintenance Procedures

JCI had contractual responsibility for maintaining the Miami airport APM system, having taken over that role from Bombardier in 2008. A JCI maintenance technician was the person who installed the jumper wire on the south train control panel about 1 week before the accident. Based on a review of log entries, such jumper wires had been used before by maintenance technicians to keep the trains running.

The NTSB is concerned about the lack of agreement, or even understanding, about the use of such jumper wires that was demonstrated by JCI maintenance technicians and managers. The maintenance technician who had installed the jumper wire stated that he was not sure what the jumper wire was for but acknowledged that it had been used before to keep trains running. The JCI site manager said the jumper wire was used to provide voltage to the hostler panel for manual operation. One maintenance technician was aware that the jumper wire, placed as it was, bypassed the vital braking system. He said he brought this to the attention of his superiors, but the significance of this finding was never acknowledged or acted upon. The JCI site manager told the NTSB that he had directed that the jumper wire not be used when the trains were in passenger service, but none of the maintenance technicians said they were aware of this directive, and all were apparently aware that the jumper wire was left in place during regular train operations. All of the information regarding the use of jumper wires was conveyed either orally or through logbook entries because no written policies or procedures were in place that addressed jumper wires or that delineated their use. The NTSB therefore concludes that JCI had no formalized procedures with regard to train maintenance and operations, with the result that the south train was allowed to operate without a vital backup safety system that could have prevented the accident. The NTSB therefore recommends that JCI implement procedures to prohibit the deactivation of safety-critical systems on fixed guideway transportation systems in passenger service on all properties maintained by JCI.

2.5 Organizational Accident Considerations

The phrase "organizational accidents"[12] refers to failures of large, complex systems because of multiple causes involving many people operating at different levels within their organizations. Organizational accidents occur when failures happen within the system safeguards (also called system barriers to failure). These failures consist of two types: (1) failures due to errors, violations, and other poor actions committed by people working in the system (termed "active failures") and (2) failures due to deficient design, supervision, maintenance, training, procedures, and other nonindividual factors (termed "latent failures"). The coincident occurrence of active failures and latent failures leads to organizational accidents.

The NTSB investigation identified several failures involved in this accident. Active failures included the installation by APM maintenance personnel of a jumper wire that bypassed the safety-critical overspeed/overshoot circuit and the failure of JCI to develop formal procedures for the proper use of jumper wires or other techniques or processes that could affect the safe operation of APM trains. Latent failures included the absence of effective safety oversight of the Miami airport APM systems by MDAD and the lack of safety oversight of fixed guideway transit systems by the state of Florida (both discussed in the section below). These active and latent failures coincided in this accident.

2.6 Safety Oversight of Miami Airport APM System

2.6.1 MDAD

Safety oversight of the APM system at Miami International Airport should have been provided by, at a minimum, MDAD and the state of Florida. The NTSB's investigation revealed, however, that neither entity was routinely providing detailed oversight with regard to safety issues.

The MDAD project manager/superintendent of contracts and construction was responsible for monitoring the safety and maintenance of the system while the MDAD Facilities Maintenance Division was responsible for oversight of the APM system contractor. Those oversight roles were largely carried out by notifying JCI maintenance technicians when a train malfunctioned and relying on those maintenance technicians to take the actions necessary to return the trains to service.

JCI had taken over as maintenance contractor for the system about 10 months before the accident. Based on maintenance records and employee interviews, the trains during that period had exhibited frequent and recurring problems that were addressed on an ad hoc basis. At no point did MDAD management evaluate the various safety risks inherent in the APM system and develop methods of managing and minimizing those risks. Nor did it seek to enforce the contract provision requiring that trains be taken out of service in the event of a malfunction that significantly degraded passenger safety.

---

[12] J. Reason, *Managing the Risks of Organizational Accidents* (Aldershot: Ashgate, 2009 [reprint]).

Risk to passengers rose to unacceptable levels when trains were allowed to operate in passenger service with the overspeed/overshoot system bypassed. However, the fact that the vital overspeed/overshoot system was being bypassed on some trains in passenger service was apparently not known by MDAD management, indicating a failure of the agency to fulfill its proper oversight role.

The NTSB concludes that the state of Florida and MDAD failed to exercise safety oversight of the Miami International Airport APM system, which resulted in trains being allowed to operate in regular passenger service with a vital safety system disabled.

The investigation also revealed other instances in which MDAD safety oversight of JCI was lacking or ineffective. For example, JCI managers told investigators that no procedures were available for testing the service and emergency braking systems on the APM trains. NTSB investigators discovered, however, that such procedures did exist and were published in the maintenance manuals for the equipment. Nonetheless, brake tests were not being routinely conducted.

Although it was found to be working properly at the time of the accident, the vital overspeed/overshoot relay that had been bypassed by the jumper wire had not been inspected in almost 7 years. JCI was unable to provide documentation regarding relay test procedures for the overspeed/overshoot relay or any other vital relays used in the APM system. Bombardier procedures required that such relays be inspected on a 4-year cycle, which is consistent with the maintenance standards within the freight and transit railroad industries. MDAD had not verified that either JCI or Bombardier conducted brake tests or tested vital relays as recommended by the equipment manufacturers.

The NTSB therefore recommends that Miami-Dade County develop and implement a system safety program plan to identify and manage safety hazards on all fixed guideway transportation systems within its jurisdiction.

2.6.2 State of Florida

The Florida DOT provides safety oversight of six fixed guideway transportation systems within the state, including APM systems at the Orlando and Tampa airports. The Florida DOT does not provide safety oversight of the APM system at Miami International Airport. In 1988, the Florida DOT asked that MDAD develop a system safety program plan for the Miami airport APM. Although MDAD acknowledged that the state partly financed the system, it declined to develop a safety plan stating that the system predated the state statute requiring such oversight.

The Florida DOT also does not provide safety oversight of the monorail APM system at Walt Disney World Resort in Lake Buena Vista, Florida, where a fatal accident occurred on July 5, 2009.[13] The state does not provide oversight because the monorail system did not receive state or FTA funding.

External safety oversight of public transportation systems is critical to identifying and correcting systemic safety risks that may not be readily apparent or may not be effectively addressed by the operator or transit agency. The NTSB believes that higher level oversight of fixed guideway transportation systems, such as the Miami airport APM system, is necessary to help promote effective risk analysis and safety management of these systems and will lead to safer travel.

2.7 Safety Oversight of U.S. APM Systems

The NTSB has long seen the need to improve the oversight of rail transit operators by state oversight agencies; however, the FTA, which requires that such an oversight agency be identified, does not, and cannot, due to its limited statutory authority, provide the oversight agency with the authority to promulgate and enforce safety regulations or standards. Therefore, except for states such as California and Massachusetts, which have provided their oversight agencies with regulatory and enforcement authority, a state oversight agency is limited in its ability to compel a rail transit agency to comply with its system safety program plan or any other FTA requirement.

To compound this deficiency, not all transit and fixed guideway systems—as is the case with the Miami airport APM—are subject even to state oversight. The state of Florida is not alone in this regard. As shown in appendix B, at least 22 other states have fixed guideway systems that fall outside the regulatory authority of the designated state oversight agencies.

The NTSB is concerned that the lack of safety oversight of some APM systems creates a situation in which adequate risk management and safety standards may not exist or may be ineffectively applied, which could lead to an inconsistent level of safety and risk management and a heightened risk to passengers. The NTSB concludes that a lack of state and Federal safety oversight of fixed guideway transit systems can permit those systems to operate with ineffective

---

[13] *Collision of Two Monorails in Walt Disney World Resort, Lake Buena Vista, Florida, July 5, 2009*, Railroad Accident Brief NTSB/RAB-11/07 (Washington, DC: National Transportation Safety Board, 2011). <http://www.ntsb.gov>.

safety standards, which could, in turn, lead to failures of safety-critical operations and procedures.

The NTSB has attempted to address the lack of safety oversight of rail transit systems by issuing a series of safety recommendations over a number of years. For example, as a result of the safety oversight issues raised in its investigation of the July 11, 2006, derailment of a Chicago Transit Authority train in Chicago, Illinois,[14] the NTSB recommended that the FTA develop and implement an action plan, including provisions for technical and financial resources as necessary, to enhance the effectiveness of state safety oversight programs, to identify safety deficiencies, and to ensure that those deficiencies are corrected.[15]

Less than a year after the accident at Miami International Airport, the NTSB investigated a much more serious accident involving a collision of two Washington Metropolitan Area Transit Authority Metrorail trains in Washington, DC.[16] Based on the findings from that investigation, as well as from its investigations of previous rail transit accidents, the NTSB concluded that the structure of the FTA's oversight process leads to inconsistent practices, inadequate standards, and marginal effectiveness with respect to the state safety oversight of rail transit systems in the United States. The NTSB, therefore, issued the following safety recommendation to the DOT:

> Continue to seek the authority to provide safety oversight of rail fixed guideway transportation systems, including the ability to promulgate and enforce safety regulations and minimum requirements governing operations, track and equipment, and signal and train control systems. (R-10-3)

In an attempt to place renewed emphasis on this important safety issue, the NTSB reiterates Safety Recommendation R-10-3 to the DOT.

On December 7, 2009, the secretary of the DOT submitted draft legislation to the Congress that, if enacted, would provide the FTA with a significant increase in its ability to provide oversight of the rail transit system. The proposed legislation would (1) authorize the secretary to establish and enforce Federal safety standards for rail transit systems that receive Federal transit assistance—effectively eliminating the statutory prohibition against imposing broad safety standards that have been in place since 1965, (2) allow states to be eligible for Federal assistance in hiring and training state oversight personnel to enforce the new Federal regulations, and (3) require the state agencies conducting oversight to be fully financially independent from the transit systems they oversee. The FTA would enforce all Federal regulations where states choose not to participate in the program or where the state program is found to lack the necessary enforcement tools. The DOT has not submitted comparable draft legislation to the current Congress. However, on March 10, 2011, Senator Barbara A. Mikulski

---

[14] *Derailment of Chicago Transit Authority Train Number 220 Between Clark/Lake and Grand/Milwaukee Stations, Chicago, Illinois, July 11, 2006,* Railroad Accident Report NTSB/RAR-07/02 (Washington, DC: National Transportation Safety Board, 2007). <http://www.ntsb.gov>.

[15] Safety Recommendations R-07-9 and -10.

[16] *Collision of Two Washington Metropolitan Area Transit Authority Metrorail Trains Near Fort Totten Station, Washington, D.C., June 22, 2009,* Railroad Accident Report NTSB/RAR-10/02 (Washington, DC: National Transportation Safety Board, 2010). <http://www.ntsb.gov>.

introduced similar legislation, titled the "National Metro Safety Act." The proposed legislation would, among other things, direct the Secretary of Transportation to develop, implement, and enforce national safety standards for transit agencies operating heavy rail on fixed guideways.

As discussed previously, about 22 states are known to have, within their jurisdictions, fixed guideway transportation systems that fall outside the regulatory authority and oversight of the designated state safety oversight agency. Other states may also have fixed guideway systems that are not subject to state safety oversight. The first step in addressing this deficiency is to identify all fixed guideway transportation systems within each state as a precursor to obtaining the regulatory authority to provide the necessary safety oversight. The NTSB, therefore, recommends that the DOT, the 50 states, and the District of Columbia work together to identify all fixed guideway transportation systems within each jurisdiction. As a followup to that effort, the NTSB recommends that each of the 50 states and the District of Columbia obtain the statutory authority to provide safety oversight of all fixed guideway transportation systems that operate within its jurisdiction, regardless of their funding authorization or the date they began operation.

3. Conclusions

3.1 Findings

1. The south train failed to make a normal deceleration and stop at its station platform berthing point because of the failure of a crystal within the program stop system module.

2. Had it not been bypassed by placement of a jumper wire as part of a troubleshooting process, the overspeed/overshoot relay on board the south train would have functioned as designed when the program stop module failed and the overspeed/overshoot system would have intervened to safely stop the train and prevent the accident.

3. Johnson Controls, Inc., had no formalized procedures with regard to train maintenance and operations, with the result that the south train was allowed to operate without a vital backup safety system that could have prevented the accident.

4. The state of Florida and the Miami-Dade Aviation Department failed to exercise safety oversight of the Miami International Airport automated people mover system, which resulted in trains being allowed to operate in regular passenger service with a vital safety system disabled.

5. A lack of state and Federal safety oversight of fixed guideway transit systems can permit those systems to operate with ineffective safety standards, which could, in turn, lead to failures of safety-critical operations and procedures.

3.2 Probable Cause

The National Transportation Safety Board determines that the probable cause of this accident was the installation by Johnson Controls, Inc., maintenance technicians of a jumper wire that prevented the overspeed/overshoot system from activating to stop the train when the crystal within the primary program stop module failed. Contributing to the accident were (1) the failure of Johnson Controls, Inc., to provide its maintenance technicians with specific procedures regarding the potential disabling of vital train control systems during passenger operations, (2) ineffective safety oversight by the Miami-Dade Aviation Department, (3) lack of adequate safety oversight of such systems by the state of Florida, and (4) lack of authority by the U.S. Department of Transportation to provide adequate safety oversight of such systems.

4. Recommendations

As a result of its investigation of this accident, the National Transportation Safety Board makes the following safety recommendations:

4.1 New Recommendations

To the U.S. Department of Transportation:

Working with the 50 states and the District of Columbia, identify all fixed guideway transportation systems within each jurisdiction. (R-11-1)

To the 50 States and the District of Columbia:

Working with the U.S. Department of Transportation, identify all fixed guideway transportation systems within your jurisdiction. (R-11-2)

Obtain the statutory authority to provide safety oversight of all fixed guideway transportation systems that operate within your jurisdiction, regardless of their funding authorization or the date they began operation. (R-11-3)

To Miami-Dade County:

Develop and implement a system safety program plan to identify and manage safety hazards on all fixed guideway transportation systems within your jurisdiction. (R-11-4)

To Johnson Controls, Inc.:

Implement procedures to prohibit the deactivation of safety-critical systems on fixed guideway transportation systems in passenger service on all properties maintained by Johnson Controls, Inc. (R-11-5)

4.2 Previously Issued Recommendation Reiterated in This Report

To the U.S. Department of Transportation:

Continue to seek the authority to provide safety oversight of rail fixed guideway transportation systems, including the ability to promulgate and enforce safety regulations and minimum requirements governing operations, track and equipment, and signal and train control systems. (R-10-3)

BY THE NATIONAL TRANSPORTATION SAFETY BOARD

DEBORAH A.P. HERSMAN
Chairman

ROBERT L. SUMWALT
Member

CHRISTOPHER A. HART
Vice Chairman

MARK R. ROSEKIND
Member

EARL F. WEENER
Member

Adopted: November 8, 2011

Vice Chairman Hart filed the following concurring statement on November 16, 2011, and was joined by Chairman Hersman and Members Sumwalt, Rosekind, and Weener.

Vice Chairman Hart, concurring:

I concur with the findings, the probable cause, and recommendations, but I would like to emphasize one aspect of one of our recommendations.

Recommendation 5, to Johnson Controls, Inc., states:

> Implement procedures to prohibit the deactivation of safety-critical systems on fixed guideway transportation systems in passenger service on all properties maintained by Johnson Controls, Inc.

As I noted in the meeting, situations may arise in which deactivation of a safety-critical system is warranted in the interests of safety, so I want to be certain that our "legislative history" of this recommendation, so to speak, includes the notion of allowing a safety-critical system to be deactivated if necessary for safety reasons, and specifies what might be required in order to do so, e.g., permission from an appropriate level manager or supervisor.

5. Appendixes

5.1 Appendix A: Investigation

The NTSB was notified of the accident on December 1, 2008. The investigator-in-charge and other members of the NTSB investigative team were launched from the headquarters office in Washington, DC, and from field offices in Atlanta, Georgia, and Gardena, California. The NTSB's investigation focused on mechanical, operations, signal and train control, and safety/oversight issues.

Parties to the investigation were the Miami-Dade Aviation Department, Johnson Controls, Inc., and Bombardier–Automated People Movers.

5.2 Appendix B: Safety Oversight Agencies for Fixed Guideway Systems

Table B-1: Safety Oversight Agencies for Fixed Guideway Systems.[a]

State	Safety Oversight Agency	Regulated APM System	Nonregulated APM System[b]
Alaska			Ketchikan-Creek
California	California Public Utilities Commission–Rail Safety Division	San Francisco Airport	Disneyland
			Getty Center
			Dana Point-Strand Beach Funicular
			California State Fair at CalExpo
Colorado	Colorado Public Utilities Commission	Denver Airport	Canon City-Royal Gorge Incline
District of Columbia	Tri-State Oversight Committee		Congressional Subways
	DC Department of Public Works		
Florida	Florida Department of Transportation–Office of Public Transportation	Orlando Airport	Miami Airport
		Tampa Airport	Zoo Miami
		Jacksonville	Walt Disney World
		Downtown Miami Metromover	
Georgia	Georgia Department of Transportation–Office of Intermodal Programs		Atlanta Hartsfield Airport
Hawaii			Pearlridge, Honolulu-SkyCab
Illinois	Regional Transportation Authority		Chicago O'Hare Airport
Indiana			Indianapolis, (Schwager Davis, Inc.)
Massachusetts	Massachusetts Department of Telecommunications and Energy		Mystic Center
Michigan	Michigan Department of Consumer and Industry Services	Downtown Detroit People Mover	Detroit Airport
Minnesota	Minneapolis-St. Paul Metropolitan Council		Minneapolis Airport
			Minnesota Zoo
Nevada	No state oversight of these systems[c]		McCarran Airport
			Bellagio
			Circus Circus
			Mandalay Bay
			MGM
			Mirage
			Primm Valley

[a] List is compiled based on available information and may not be complete.

[b] Includes systems where the state oversight agency, if any, is unknown. Some systems may be regulated by the state elevator inspection agency.

[c] Regulation of these systems is by the Clark County Building department.

State	Safety Oversight Agency	Regulated APM System	Nonregulated APM System
New Jersey	New Jersey Department of Transportation Division of Motor Vehicles		Newark Liberty Airport-AirTrain
			Ocean City-Gillians Wonderland Pier
New York	New York Public Transportation Safety Board Passenger & Freight Safety Division	Airtrain JFK	
		Bronx Zoo	
North Carolina			Duke Hospital
Ohio	Ohio Department of Transportation – Office of Public Transportation		Cincinnati Airport (Kentucky)
Pennsylvania	Pennsylvania Department of Transportation–Bureau of Public Transportation		Pittsburgh Airport
			Hershey Park
			Dutch Wonderland
			Pittsburgh–Duquesne Incline
			Pittsburgh–Monongahela incline
Tennessee	Tennessee Department of Transportation–Office of Public Transportation		Mudd Island, Memphis
			Chattanooga–Lookout Mountain Incline
Texas	Texas Department of Transportation–Public Transportation Division		Dallas-Fort Worth Airport
			George Bush Intercontinental Airport
			Las Colinas, Dallas
			Dallas Zoo
Virginia	Tri-State Oversight Committee c/o Virginia Department of Rail & Public Transportation		Old Dominion University
			Washington Dulles Airport–AeroTrain
Washington	Washington Department of Transportation–Public Transportation and Rail		Seattle-Tacoma Airport
			Seattle Center Monorail
West Virginia			Morgantown